WORLD ALMANAC®
LIBRARY OF THE
Middle East

PEOPLES
AND CULTURES
of the Middle East

Nicola Barber

Academic Consultant:
William Ochsenwald
Professor of History, Virginia Polytechnic Institute
and State University

WORLD ALMANAC® LIBRARY

Please visit our website at: www.garethstevens.com
For a free color catalog describing World Almanac® Library's list of high-quality books
and multimedia programs, call 1-800-848-2928 (USA) or 1-800-387-3178 (Canada).
World Almanac® Library's Fax: (414) 332-3567.

Library of Congress Cataloging-in-Publication Data

Barber, Nicola.
  Peoples and cultures of the Middle East / Nicola Barber.
    p. cm. — (World Almanac Library of the Middle East)
  Includes bibliographical references and index.
  ISBN-10: 0-8368-7337-8 — ISBN-13: 978-0-8368-7337-5 (lib. bdg.)
  ISBN-10: 0-8368-7344-0 — ISBN-13: 978-0-8368-7344-3 (softcover)
  1. Middle East. I. Title. II. Series.
  DS44.B214   2007
  956—dc22   2006014033

First published in 2007 by
World Almanac® Library
A Member of the WRC Media Family of Companies
330 West Olive Street, Suite 100
Milwaukee, WI 53212, USA

This edition © 2007 by World Almanac® Library.

Produced by Discovery Books
Editors: Geoff Barker, Amy Bauman, Paul Humphrey, and Sarah Jameson
Series designer: Sabine Beaupré
Designer and page production: Ian Winton
Photo researchers: Sarah Jameson and Rachel Tisdale
Maps and diagrams: Stefan Chabluk and Ian Winton
Academic Consultant: William Ochsenwald,
     Professor of History, Virginia Polytechnic Institute and
     State University
World Almanac® Library editorial direction: Mark J. Sachner
World Almanac® Library editor: Alan Wachtel
World Almanac® Library art direction: Tammy West
World Almanac® Library production: Jessica Morris

Picture credits: cover: Rohan/Stone/Getty Images; p. 5: Sabah Arar/AFP/Getty Images;
p. 7. Behrouz Mehri/AFP/Getty Images; p. 9: Norbert Schiller/Getty Images; p. 11: Brian
Hendler/Getty Images; p. 13: Ahmad Khateib/Getty Images; p. 14 Gali Tibbon/AFP/Getty
Images; p. 17: Jorgen Schytte/Still Pictures; p. 21: Ramzi Haidar/AFP/Getty Images; p. 23:
Marco Di Lauro/Getty Images; p. 25: Salah Malkawi/Getty Images; p. 27: Tim Graham/Getty
Images; p. 29: Uriel Sinai/Getty Images; p. 31: Behrouz Mehri/AFP/Getty Images; p. 33:
The Trustees of the Chester Beatty Library, Dublin/The Bridgeman Art Library ; p. 34:
Osterreichische Nationalbibliothek, Vienna, Austria/Archives Charmet/The Bridgeman
Art Library; p. 37: World Religions Photo Library/Osborne; p. 38: Ed Kashi; p. 41: Ed Kashi;
p. 43: Jamal Aruri/AFP/Getty Images.

Printed in the United States of America

1 2 3 4 5 6 7 8 9 10 09 08 07 06

CONTENTS

Cover: *A bagel stall attracts customers at the Damascus Gate in the Old City, Jerusalem, Israel.*

The Middle East

The term *Middle East* has a long and complex history. It was originally used by the British in the nineteenth century to describe the area between the Near East (those lands gathered around the eastern end of the Mediterranean Sea) and Britain's empire in India. This area included Persia (later Iran), the **Mesopotamian provinces** of the **Ottoman Empire** (later Iraq), and the eastern half of Saudi Arabia. It was centered on the Persian Gulf.

In this series, the Middle East is taken to include the following fifteen countries: Libya and Egypt in north Africa, along with Israel, Lebanon, Syria, Jordan, Iraq, and Iran, and

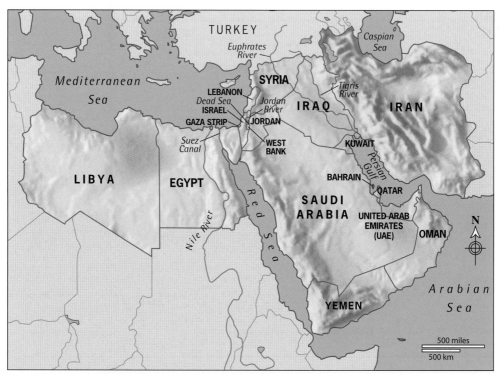

This map shows the fifteen countries of the Middle East that will be discussed in this book, as well as the West Bank and the Gaza Strip.

An Arab coffee seller holds a bronze coffee pot and the small cups in which coffee is traditionally served in Arab cultures.

the **Arabian Peninsula** countries of Bahrain, Kuwait, Saudi Arabia, United Arab Emirates (UAE), Oman, Yemen, and Qatar. It also includes the disputed Arab Palestinian territories—the **West Bank** and **Gaza Strip**—which have had varying degrees of autonomy under Israeli occupation since 1967.

Why is this region important? Two reasons stand out. One, the Middle East was the original source of civilization, and the three great religions of Christianity, **Judaism**, and **Islam** all grew up there. The area includes Israel, the state of the Jewish people, and a significant proportion of the world's **Muslims**. Two, the Middle East has two-thirds of the fuel that keeps the rest of the world running—oil. For these two reasons alone, the affairs of the Middle East—its peoples and resources, religions and politics, revolutions and wars—are of vital interest to everyone on the planet.

This book looks at the peoples and cultures of the Middle East. The ethnic and religious background of the Middle East population is described and the differences between rural and city life are discussed. Family life, the region's wide variety of foods, and, finally, the languages, literature, and arts of the region are examined.

CHAPTER 1

People of the Middle East

The people of the Middle East have a wide variety of beliefs, customs, languages, religions, and traditions, and the region is one of rich ethnic diversity. Most people in the region are Muslim, yet it also includes major Jewish and Christian communities. Every country in the Middle East has its own unique ethnic and religious makeup, which is a result of its history and culture. For example, Saudi Arabia, the birthplace of Islam, has a largely Arab population and 100 percent of its citizens are Muslim. In contrast, the country of Israel has a largely Jewish population, while in the Gulf state of Kuwait, native Kuwaitis are outnumbered by "foreign nationals"—people from other countries who have come to Kuwait to live and work.

Ethnicity

Ethnicity refers to a way of grouping people according to descent, shared customs, beliefs, and often language. In many cases, these characteristics have been passed down through countless generations. In the Middle East, examples of ethnic groups include the Arabs, the Kurds, the Jews, and the Persians (Iranians). Frequently, many different ethnic groups are found within the borders of a single country. For example, Iran's population includes Persians, Kurds, Azeris (of Turkish origin), Arabs, Lurs (part Persian, part Arab), and Gilakis (part Persian, part Turkish). Similarly, many ethnic groups spread geographically across more than one country. For example, the Kurds inhabit a broad stretch of land that extends across Turkey, Syria, Iraq, and Iran.

A Muslim woman helps her daughter to dress before weekly Friday prayers in Tehran, Iran. In the Middle East, the vast majority of people are Muslims.

Islam

Religion plays a central role in the lives of millions of people in the Middle East. The region was the birthplace of three major world religions—Christianity, Judaism, and Islam. Today, Islam has the largest number of followers in the Middle East—about 94 percent of the region's population is Muslim. Islam started in the seventh century A.D. when the **Prophet** Muhammad is believed to have received a series of messages, or revelations, from God (known in Arabic as Allah) in a cave just outside Mecca, in present-day Saudi Arabia. Muhammad began to teach the central message of Islam, submission to God, which is summed up in the Muslim declaration of faith, the *shahadah*: "There is no god except Allah; Muhammad is the Messenger of Allah."

According to Islamic belief, the Prophet Muhammad was the last in a series of prophets to teach the message of God that included Ibrahim (Abraham), Musa (Moses), and Isa (Jesus). Muslims believe that Muhammad was the messenger for God's final and complete teaching for his people, brought together in the Muslim holy book, the Koran. Islam, therefore, has strong links with both Judaism and Christianity, and Muslims call both Jews and Christians "people of the book" because they too worship one God and trace their ancestry back through the prophets to Abraham.

Sunni and Shi'a

Today, the vast majority of Muslims in the Middle East belong to one of two major groups within Islam: Sunni and Shi'a. The origins of these groups can be traced back to the years after the death of the Prophet Muhammad in A.D. 632. Some people thought that the prophet's successor as leader of the Muslims should be a member of his close family, his cousin and son-in-law Ali. Those who supported Ali became known as the Shi'at Ali, which means "the party of Ali," and are today called Shi'as (or Shi'ites). Others believed that Muhammad's successor should be the person best able to uphold the Sunnah—the customs and practices of the prophet, and they became known as Sunnis (or Sunnites).

Today, Sunni Muslims account for about 90 percent of the Muslim population worldwide. In the Middle East, Sunni Muslims make up the majority of the Muslim population except in Iran, Iraq, Bahrain, and Lebanon, where there are large numbers of Shi'a Muslims.

Ibadi Muslims

The majority of Muslims in Oman belong to yet another group known as the Ibadites. Oman is the only country in which this form of Islam is dominant. Ibadism was founded less than fifty years after the death of the Prophet Muhammad, so, along with the Sunni and Shi'a **sects**, it is one of the earliest forms of Islam. One belief of Ibadism is that the leader, or imam, of the Ibadis should be the most worthy person for the office, and that if he proves himself unworthy he can be replaced.

Ethnicity and Religion

While shared beliefs is one of the bonds that hold ethnic groups together, the relationship between ethnicity and religion is not always clear cut. For example, the vast majority of Arabs, one of the main ethnic groups of the Middle East, are Muslims. Yet there are also millions of Arab Christians and thousands of Arab Jews. In the Middle East, significant communities of Arab Christians live in Egypt, Syria, and Lebanon, and small communities in the Gaza Strip and West Bank. And before 1948, hundreds of thousands of Jews lived in the Arab countries of the Middle East, but most left their countries and resettled in Israel when that country was created. Today, only a few thousand now remain in the region outside of Israel, mainly in Iraq, Syria, and Egypt.

Copts

In Egypt, Arab Christians, known as Copts, make up about 6 percent of the population. The word *Copt* is derived from the Arabic *qibt*, which in turn comes from the Greek word for "Egyptian." Christianity arrived in Egypt very early when St. Mark, one of the writers of the New Testament of the Bible, came to the country to preach in about A.D. 40. Coptic Christianity formed a separate branch of Christianity in A.D. 451, and this branch remains separate today, with its own **patriarch**.

Coptic priests and pilgrims take part in a procession through the village of Deir Abu Hennis in Egypt. Coptic Christians believe this village was visited by the Holy Family (Mary, Joseph, and Jesus) during their flight to Egypt.

Arabs

The Arabs originally came from Arabia, the peninsula of land that is bounded by the Red Sea on one side and the Persian Gulf on the other. Traditionally, many Arabs were **nomads**, known as Bedouin. Today, an Arab is usually defined as someone who speaks the Arabic language, lives in an Arabic-speaking country, and has an understanding and knowledge of the history and customs of the Arabic people.

Most Arabs are Muslims. The religion of Islam spread quickly across the Arabian peninsula after the death of the Prophet Muhammad, and Arab Muslim armies soon took control of lands to the north, west, and east of the peninsula, taking their religion with them. The Arab **Umayyad** and **Abbasid dynasties** continued this expansion until the Islamic world reached from present-day Morocco on the northwest coast of Africa to Afghanistan in the east. Today, the "Arab world" is usually said to include nearly all Middle Eastern countries and North Africa.

Even non-Arab countries in the Middle East have large Arab minorities. About one million Arabs live in Israel (about 20 percent of the population), while in Iran only 3 percent of the population is Arab.

Kurds

The Kurds live in a mostly high, mountainous region that runs across Turkey, Syria, Iraq, and Iran and was historically known as Kurdistan. Population estimates number the Kurds in this area at about 25 million. The vast majority of Kurds are Sunni Muslims, and they speak their own language, Kurdish, which is related to Persian. Most Kurds speak two main **dialects** of Kurdish—Sorani (in Iraq and Iran) and Kurmanji (in Turkey and Syria)—but there are many other minor dialects as well, so it is quite possible for one Kurdish speaker not to understand another. The Kurds have long fought for their own independent country and have

A Kurdish State

"I don't think that Kurds will abandon their aim of establishing an independent Kurdish state."

Jalal Talabani, president of Iraq and founder of the Patriotic Union of Kurdistan.

experienced repression and brutality as a result, particularly in Turkey, Iraq, and Iran.

Jews

The Jews trace their ancestry back thousands of years to the Hebrews, an ancient people who lived in what is now Israel. The Jews consider the founder of their religion to be Abraham, and they believe that God made a covenant, or agreement, with Abraham that marked the Jews as God's "Chosen People" and gave them special responsibilities and duties. Today, Jews live in countries all over the world, but the Jewish community is united by common heritage and its faith. The country with the largest Jewish population is the United States (with about 5.5 million Jews), but Israel has the second largest Jewish population. The majority of Israel's Jewish population is made up of immigrants and descendants of immigrants from all over the world, with around 33 percent of Israeli Jews born in Israel itself.

A boy reads from the Torah, the Jewish holy book, in front of the Western Wall in Jerusalem, one of the holiest sites for Jews. The boy is celebrating his Bar Mitzvah, marking his entry into adulthood.

Ashkenazic, Sephardic, and Mizrahi Jews

The three main groups of Jews in Israel are the Ashkenazim, Sephardim, and Mizrahi. The Ashkenazim are Jews who trace their ancestry back to central and eastern Europe (*Ashkenazim* comes from the Hebrew word for "Germany"). Yiddish, a mixture of German and Hebrew, is the traditional language of the Ashkenazim, and Ashkenazic customs, religious practices, and food differ from those of the Sephardic Jews.

The Sephardim are those Jews who were originally from Spain and Portugal (*Sephardim* comes from the Hebrew word for "Spain"). In 1492, the Roman Catholic Church expelled the Sephardim from Spain, and many fled to the Ottoman Empire (Turkey and Greece), Yemen, and North Africa. The Sephardim also have their own customs and their own language—Ladino, a mixture of Spanish and Hebrew. The Mizrahi are Jews who descended from the Jewish communities of the Middle East. Traditionally these people spoke Hebrew mixed with various Arabic dialects.

After the creation of Israel in 1948, there were tensions between the established community of the Ashkenazim and the Sephardim and Mizrahi Jews who were mostly from Africa and the Middle East. The Ashkenazim held most of the political power, which left many Sephardim and Mizrahi Jews feeling as if they were being treated as Israel's second-class citizens.

The Arab-Israeli Conflict

Jewish settlers began to arrive in Palestine in the early 1880s. In 1947, the United Nations (UN) put forward a plan to divide the territory of Palestine, creating two separate states: one an Arab country and one a Jewish country. The Jews accepted the proposal. The Arabs—who made up 65 percent of the population but had been offered less than half of the land—refused it, and war followed. The state of Israel was declared in 1948. Under attack from its Arab neighbors, Israel extended its control over more territory during further wars in 1956, 1967, and 1973.

Today, this situation is changing as more Sephardim and Mizrahi hold leading positions in the Israeli government.

Refugees

In the face of the creation of Israel in 1948 and the war that followed, 711,000 Palestinian Arabs left their homes, according to UN figures. Some of these people became refugees, living in camps along the West Bank and Gaza. Others were taken in by the neighboring Arab countries of Jordan, Syria, and Lebanon. Today, the UN estimates the number of Palestinian refugees to be 3.7 million, many of whom continue to live in refugee camps. The future of these people is one of the main problems in the negotiations between Israel and the Palestinians.

Racism

"There's a lot of racism against Arabs inside Israel, and there's a lot of racism by Arabs against Israeli Jews."

Robert Fisk, British journalist.

Palestinian children play in the dusty street of a refugee camp in Gaza. There are over 900,000 Palestinian refugees registered with the United Nations in the Gaza Strip alone.

CHAPTER 2

Rural Life

Since agriculture began in the Middle East, the need for water has been the single most important concern of the region's farmers. The whole region has extremely low average rainfall, and areas of cultivation and population closely follow coasts, rivers, and the scattered **oases** where water can be found. Over the centuries, people have devised methods of **irrigation** to make the best use of the water that is available. The great civilizations that grew up along the banks of the Tigris and Euphrates rivers and along the Nile River, relied on sophisticated methods of water extraction, storage, and distribution for their success. Today, water supply and water management remain vital issues for Middle Eastern countries.

An Israeli Bedouin leads his camel after a race in the Negev desert in southern Israel. Although not as important as they once were, camels still play a part in Bedouin life.

The Bedouin

The vast interior of the Arabian peninsula is arid desert. It is largely uninhabited, with an average **population density** of less than two people per square mile. Yet one group of people who did learn how to survive in this harsh environment were the Bedouins. The name *Bedoui* comes from the Arabic *badu*, meaning "people of the desert."

> "Truth may walk through the world unarmed."
>
> *Bedouin proverb.*

Bedouins are Arabs who have traditionally lived their lives as nomads—moving from one place to another with their herds of animals. The key to this way of life has been the camel, an animal very well adapted to extreme desert conditions, although Bedouins also keep sheep and goats, and raise highly prized Arabian horses for racing and hunting.

In the past, Bedouins lived in tents woven from goat or camel hair. During the fiercely hot summer months (June to September), they kept their herds close to sources of water. But during the cooler winter months, they moved deep into the desert in search of grazing areas for their animals. Today, it is estimated that Bedouin people make up at most 10 percent of the Arab population of the Middle East. They live in the desert regions of the Arabian Peninsula, Egypt's Sinai Peninsula, Israel, Jordan, Saudi Arabia, and elsewhere. Many have abandoned their nomadic ways of life for more settled lifestyles in towns and villages. Some continue to live as nomads but may have modern tents and use trucks to move their herds from one place to another.

Bedouins have increasingly come under pressure from governments of countries in the Middle East to settle in certain places. For example, in the Negev desert in southern Israel, the Israeli government wants to move the 110,000-strong Bedouin population into seven towns that have been built for this purpose. To this end, Israeli forces have destroyed many homes of Negev Bedouin that the government does not recognize as legal settlements. Many Bedouins have resisted this resettlement, as the towns are some of the poorest places in the country, and they continue to claim the right to live in their desert lands.

Rural Communities

Until recently, the vast majority of people in the Middle East lived in villages in rural areas where they grew crops to support themselves and their families. Today, there has been a massive increase in **urbanization** as people move from the country to towns and cities.

One reason for this **migration** is that poverty is more widespread in rural than in urban areas. For poor farmers who depend on their crops and animals as the main sources of their livelihood, life can be hard. In many places, young men in particular have left their villages and their families' fields to look for better lives in the cities. Some travel to other countries in the Middle East to find higher-paid work and send money to their families back home.

Nevertheless, in a country such as Egypt, agriculture continues to employ one-third of the population, and more than half of the population lives in rural areas. Today, much of the farming is heavily mechanized, with machines used for pumping water for irrigation and for working the land. In contrast, some of the small oil-rich states along the Persian Gulf—the so-called Gulf states—have virtually no rural communities at all. Before the discovery of oil, the inhabitants of Qatar, a desert country and one of the wealthiest countries in the region, were Bedouin nomads. Wealth from oil has meant that Qatar is now a nation of city dwellers, with 90 percent of the population living in the capital, Doha, on its east coast.

The Berbers

The Berbers are a partly nomadic group of the Middle East. While a large number of Berbers live in Algeria, Tunisia, and Morocco, Berbers are also found in Libya and Egypt. The Berbers descend from the people who were living in north Africa before the Muslim invasions in the seventh century. Today, most Berbers are Sunni Muslims. While many Berbers are farmers, some nomadic Berber communities remain, moving from place to place with their herds in the Sahara.

A vet holds bottles of drugs for vaccinating sheep in an Egyptian village. The coarse wool from Egyptian sheep is mostly used for making rugs and similar items.

Less than 2 percent of the country's land is used for agriculture, which relies heavily on expensive irrigation.

Kibbutz Life

Kibbutz (plural kibbutzim) is the Hebrew word for "gathering" or "community," and it describes a type of rural communal settlement in Israel. The first kibbutz was set up in the early 20th century. The founding principle was one of individual equality, in which people gave according to their abilities and took according to their needs. Today, there are over 260 kibbutzim in Israel, with communities ranging from about 100 to more than 1,000 people. In the first kibbutzim, the majority of the work was agricultural. Today, only about 15 percent of people who work in kibbutzim are engaged in agriculture; the remainder work in industry and services.

CHAPTER 3

City Life

Many cities of the Middle East are the products of long and fascinating histories. For example, Cairo, the capital of Egypt, is a vast, modern, bustling city that still has distinct ancient Christian and Islamic quarters. Jerusalem, in Israel, is sacred to Jews, Christians, and Muslims, and has a diverse population as a result.

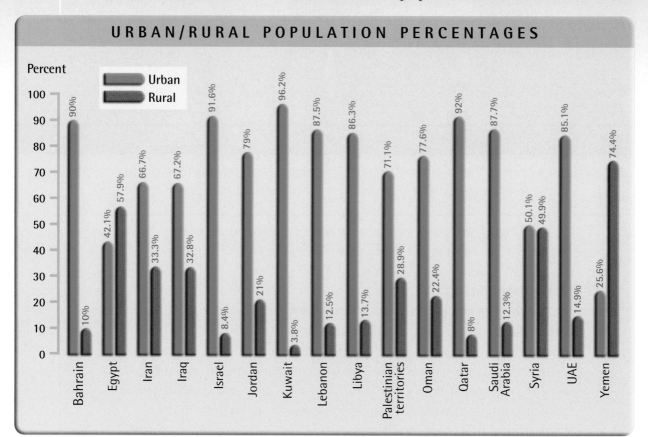

URBAN/RURAL POPULATION PERCENTAGES

Percent

Urban
Rural

Country	Urban	Rural
Bahrain	90%	10%
Egypt	42.1%	57.9%
Iran	66.7%	33.3%
Iraq	67.2%	32.8%
Israel	91.6%	8.4%
Jordan	79%	21%
Kuwait	96.2%	3.8%
Lebanon	87.5%	12.5%
Libya	86.3%	13.7%
Palestinian territories	71.1%	28.9%
Oman	77.6%	22.4%
Qatar	92%	8%
Saudi Arabia	87.7%	12.3%
Syria	50.1%	49.9%
UAE	85.1%	14.9%
Yemen	25.6%	74.4%

Source: United Nations, 2003

This bar chart shows the difference in urban and rural populations in the Middle East. The majority of people live in towns and cities, with just two countries, Egypt and Yemen, having a larger rural than urban population.

Many of these cities share one common characteristic—rapid growth. Since the 1950s, the rate of urbanization has sped up. For example, the population of the metropolitan area of Cairo nearly doubled between 1970 and 2005, growing from five million to almost ten million people, and it is expected to reach about fourteen million by 2015. The city has one of the highest population densities in the world.

The arrival of so many people has put a great strain on housing and services such as education and health in many cities. In Cairo, a poor family may live in one room in an overcrowded apartment building, often sharing a toilet and a single water faucet with many other families. Other families build illegal housing for themselves without any access to services such as clean water or sewage disposal.

Emigration and Immigration

The reason behind urbanization in the Gulf states has been great wealth—the riches that resulted from the discovery of huge oil deposits in the middle of the twentieth century. This oil wealth has drawn thousands of workers into the Gulf states from other countries in the Middle East and from countries beyond. In Kuwait, Kuwaitis are outnumbered by foreign nationals from countries as far away as India and Pakistan. Similarly, in the United Arab Emirates, Emiris make up only a small percentage of the population.

Israel is a country that has been largely built on immigration, as Jewish people from all over the world have settled there. In some cases, entire Jewish communities from a particular place moved to Israel at the same time. In 1949–1950, fears of persecution in Yemen led Jews to use a secret operation code-named "Magic Carpet" to airlift thousands of Jews out of the country to Israel. Similar secret airlift operations were mounted in 1984–1985 and in 1991 to rescue Ethiopian Jews (Falashas) and bring them to Israel. During the 1990s, Israel experienced high levels of immigration from the former republics of the Soviet Union (USSR). The arrival of hundreds of thousands of people put great pressure on Israel's government to provide housing and jobs and caused tension between established communities and the new immigrants in many Israeli cities.

Cities of the Middle East

The following three examples give a flavor of the rich variety of peoples living in the cities of the Middle East:

Jerusalem

Jerusalem, the capital of the state of Israel, has a population of over 693,000 people, of whom 67 percent are Jews and 33 percent are Muslims and Christians. The city is divided into two parts, East and West Jerusalem, and its communities are largely segregated according to their religion. West Jerusalem is home to mostly Jewish families, while East Jerusalem, which includes the Old City, is inhabited by the city's Muslim and Christian residents, as well as some Jews. In this city, which is holy to three religions (Christianity, Islam, and Judaism), there are three different holy days in the week—Friday for the Muslim community, Saturday for the Jews, and Sunday for the Christians.

Tehran

The metropolis of Tehran, which is the capital of Iran, has a population of about eleven million people. The city sits at the foot of the impressive Alborz mountains. The mixture of peoples living in the city reflects the ethnic diversity of the country as a whole. The majority are Persians, the native people of Iran, but 25 percent of the city's population are Azeris, the

Mecca

As the birthplace of the Prophet Muhammad, Mecca, Saudi Arabia, is the holiest city of Islam. It is the focus of the **Hajj,** the annual pilgrimage that all Muslims try to make at least once in their lifetimes. It also marks the direction in which all Muslims, no matter where they are in the world, turn to pray. At the center of the city lies the huge Great **Mosque,** which surrounds the **Ka'bah,** the sacred shrine of Islam. Non-Muslims are not allowed to enter Mecca, but every year, millions of Muslim pilgrims fill the city during the time of the Hajj.

This picture taken in 2001, shows rebuilding work in downtown Beirut after the destruction caused by the country's civil war. As well as being Lebanon's capital city, Beirut is the country's main seaport.

name given to Turks from the Republic of Azerbaijan to the north, and there are also Kurds and Gilakis, who are people of mixed Turkish and Persian origin. While the vast majority of the city's inhabitants are Shi'a Muslims, small Christian, Jewish, and **Zoroastrian** communities also exist.

Beirut

Beirut is the capital of Lebanon and has an estimated population of more than 1.5 million people. This beautiful city, which was a major tourist and commercial center, became a war zone when civil war broke out in Lebanon in 1975 between Christians and Muslims. The city was divided between its Christian inhabitants in the east and its Muslim inhabitants in the west. By the end of the war in 1989, much of the city lay in ruins. Today, a massive rebuilding program is taking place, and the city is slowly becoming attractive to businesses and tourists again. Its population is still very mixed—including Sunni Muslims, Shi'a Muslims, and Christians of various sects—but these groups now live together in relative peace.

CHAPTER 4

Family Life

The family is very important in Middle Eastern society. Traditionally, the family centered around a father, whose role was to provide for his wife and children, and a mother, who ran the household and cared for the children. Today, these traditional roles are being challenged by many aspects of modern living. In many countries, better education and more independence has led women to take a more active part in life outside the home. In other cases, men travel abroad for work, taking them far away from their families leaving the women to fulfill the new roles found in managing the household.

A Patrilineal Society

For many families, the family unit extends far beyond the core of father, mother, and children. Grandparents, uncles, aunts, and cousins—the extended family—may live close to each other and play a large part in each others' everyday lives. Middle Eastern families trace their descendants through the male side of the family. This is known as patrilineal descent. For example, in an Arab family, sons are named by their relationship with their father. The king and chief minister of Saudi Arabia is Abdallah bin Abd al-Aziz. He is the "son of" (bin) Abd al-Aziz. Patrilineal descent is more than simply passing on a name. Land and wealth are passed on down the male line, and male members of the same family often share business interests and rely on each other for help and support.

Marriage

Marriage is important in the Jewish, Christian, and Muslim religions, and it plays a central role in Middle Eastern society. Marriage is often viewed as more than the joining of two individuals—it is a way of bringing two families together and strengthening family bonds. Traditionally, many Muslims marry within their own extended families; for example, it is very common for cousins to marry each other. Also, parents often arrange marriages for their children, although this practice is changing in some countries where young people are being given more freedom to decide for themselves.

Before the marriage ceremony can take place, Muslim families often engage in extended negotiations about the *mahr*, the Arabic word for "**dowry**." A dowry is a sum of money, or equivalent wealth that is given by the groom's family to the bride. In practice, a proportion of the *mahr* usually goes to the bride's father, but it is also meant to provide for the bride if the marriage does not work out.

In both Muslim and Jewish marriage ceremonies, the bride and groom sign a marriage contract. In many religions, the marriage ceremony is followed by celebrations, often with feasts, singing, and dancing. After the marriage, it is usual for the bride to go and live with her husband as part of his extended family.

The **Koran** allows a Muslim man to have up to four wives as long as he can provide equally for all of them. In fact, this practice is not common except in the Gulf states and Saudi Arabia.

A family celebrates the marriage of a young couple in Iraq. Since the first Gulf War (1991), hard economic conditions in the country have meant that dowries are difficult to raise. There are now around one million Iraqi women over the age of 35 who remain unmarried.

Islamic Houses

The importance of the household unit, and the way in which households are organized in Islamic life, is reflected in the house designs found in many Middle Eastern cities.

Traditionally, houses have been built around a central courtyard with high outside walls. Often these walls are either blank or have a few small windows, giving complete privacy to the household within. In hot climates, this also has the advantage of keeping the house cool in the hot summer months and retaining heat during the colder winter months. One door into the house leads to a public room, used by the men of the household to receive and entertain guests. The women's quarters, called the **harem**, are separate. In many cases, rooms off different sides of the courtyard provide accommodation for the various parts of the extended family.

Traditions of Hospitality

The people of the Middle East are well-known for their traditions of hospitality—welcoming strangers as guests into their homes. These traditions are deep-rooted in their society and continue to this day. They stem from the struggle to survive in the harsh environment of the Middle East. In the searing heat of the desert, if a stranger was refused food and drink it was quite likely that he or she would die. Thus, mutual help and support were vital for survival in such extreme conditions, and it was from these conditions that the traditions of welcoming guests grew up in the Jewish, Christian, and Muslim religions.

Ways of welcoming guests vary from country to country, and from people to people. In general, guests are given the best seat in the house and are served first. When a guest leaves, he or she is accompanied to the door and often beyond. It is very common for coffee to be served to show that a guest is welcome and honored. If a guest is given food, he or she will be offered the tastiest morsels, and it is considered to be a compliment to the host to take a second helping.

A woman looks over her balcony in the ancient city of Basra, in southern Iraq. Many of Basra's old houses have beautiful wooden balconies like this.

The Sheikh's Son

In Bedouin society, it was the tradition for hospitality to be offered for up to three days. During those three days, a guest was under his host's protection. An Arab folktale tells of a man who killed an opponent and then took refuge in a nearby tent, only to discover that his host was the dead man's father. The father observed the customs of hospitality and protection for three days, after which the guest was obliged to leave and the father was free to pursue the murderer and avenge his son's death.

Muslim Women in the Middle East

Throughout their lives, most Muslim women in the Middle East are far more closely tied to the household and the family than their husbands, fathers, or brothers. While men's lives focus on going out to work and going to the mosque to pray, women's lives generally revolve around the home. These differences are reinforced from an early age, and the birth of a boy baby may still be a greater cause for celebration than the birth of a girl baby.

Particularly in rural areas, Muslim girls are taught to do household jobs from a young age, while their brothers are more likely to be taken out with their fathers. Many poor parents see little need to educate their daughters beyond elementary school, and **literacy** levels are still much lower for women than for men in the region.

In general, life for women in the Middle East has been difficult. The degree of difficulty from one country to another varies, however, and the situation is changing. On the one hand, honor killings—when a woman who is considered to have brought shame on her family is killed in retribution—are still reported in countries such as Jordan. In Saudi Arabia, due to the strict interpretation of Islamic law (called *sharia*), women are not allowed to vote, drive a car, or hold public office. They are permitted to do only certain jobs—mainly working as teachers or nurses—and are not allowed to travel unaccompanied on a train or bus. Women such as the Egyptian Nawal El Saadawi have risked their lives and endured terms of imprisonment in order to speak out about the situation of women in the Middle East. On the other hand, however, women do play a part in the political and professional lives of Middle Eastern countries. In Jordan, for example, women hold important ministry posts. And, in 2005, Kuwaiti women won a long battle for the right to vote and stand as candidates in their country's elections.

Wearing the Veil

The Koran states that women should dress modestly and cover themselves from the ankles to the neck when they are outside the home. Interpretations of this law have led to a wide variety of dress styles in Islamic countries. In Saudi Arabia, when outside the privacy of their homes, women must wear the *abaya*, a long, loose robe, and a head covering. Some women also wear a face veil, or *niqab*. In Iran, women are also obliged by law to cover themselves. Some wear a *chador*—a long black cloak that covers the wearer from head to toe; others wear full-length skirts or trousers and a long coat called a *roupush*. All women wear headscarves. In countries such as Egypt and Turkey, many Muslim women wear more Western styles of dress. However, even in countries where they are not obliged to do so, many Muslim women choose to wear a head covering and modest clothing on their bodies to conform to their religious beliefs.

This woman is wearing the *abaya* to go out shopping in Kuwait City. Traditionally, the *abaya* is black in color and worn by girls from around the age of 12 onward.

CHAPTER 5

Food

The food of the Middle East varies according to the traditions and cultures of its people. However, certain staple foods appear in the cuisines of all the countries of the region, including many different types of bread, meat (mainly lamb or chicken), chickpeas, beans and lentils, yogurt and honey, mint and parsley. Lebanon has a reputation for having the finest cuisine in the region, while Iran has its own distinctive traditions of cooking that are quite different from other Middle Eastern countries.

People in most countries of the Middle East consume far less fast food than people in Western countries. The exception to this is Saudi Arabia, where the popularity of American-style junk food has resulted in serious problems with obesity. A Middle Eastern breakfast often consists of bread and cheese and the main meal of the day, lunch, is usually eaten at home.

Religion and Food

The Jewish and Islamic religions both lay down strict rules about food. For Jews, food must be *kosher*, meaning "allowed" or "suitable." Pork is forbidden, as Jews may not eat any mammal that does not both chew the cud and have cloven hooves. And among birds, only certain kinds, such as chicken, duck, and turkey, may be made kosher. Jews may only eat fish that have fins and scales. Other laws govern the way in which animals are slaughtered for eating, as well as prohibiting the consumption of meat and milky foods together. Pork is also forbidden for Muslims, as is alcohol, and Islam lays down laws about the slaughter of animals for food as well. Food that is permissible for Muslims under Islamic law is *halal*.

In Israel, a Jewish baker prepares a special kind of bread called *matzo* for the festival of Pesach (Passover). Matzo is made from plain flour and water and, unlike ordinary bread, contains no yeast to make it rise.

Food from street stalls is popular and delicious, and includes *falafel* (known as *ta'amiyya* in Egypt), which is mashed chickpeas or beans and spices rolled into a ball and fried; *kofta*, which is ground meat and spices cooked on a skewer; and kebabs, which consist of pieces of lamb cooked on a skewer over a grill. Puddings in the Middle East are very sweet and are often made from layers of pastry soaked in honey, syrup, or rose water.

Drinks

Tea and coffee are the main drinks throughout the Middle East. Tea is drunk strong and without milk, and coffee is usually served very strong and thick in small cups. Arab or Bedouin coffee is often flavored with cardamom, a herb of the ginger family. It is served in tiny cups and poured from a brass coffee pot. It is considered polite to have three or four cups before refusing the offer of a refill. Throughout the region, people make the most of the fresh fruit that is available, and delicious freshly squeezed fruit drinks are available from many street vendors. Although alcohol is forbidden for Muslims, it is freely available in some countries in the Middle East. In others, such as Iran and Saudi Arabia, it is strictly prohibited.

National Dishes

Many countries have their own special "national" dishes. In Egypt, *kushari*, a mixture of pasta, rice, and lentils, topped with tomatoes, onions, and chilies, is very popular. In Syria, *maqlubbeh*, which is made from steamed rice with eggplant, tomatoes, and pine nuts, is a local specialty. In Yemen, *salta* is a meat stew with vegetables and the herb fenugreek.

The national dish of Jordan, *mensaf*, was originally a Bedouin dish. It is made up of a mound of rice topped with spicy lamb that has been cooked on a spit with pine nuts. Traditionally, this meal was served on one large plate and the head of the lamb was placed on the top. The greatest delicacies, the lamb's eyes, were saved for honored guests. The tongue was considered the next most delicious part.

Lebanese Delights

The cuisine of Lebanon combines Middle Eastern and Mediterranean traditions, and is generally regarded as the finest in the Middle East. A typical meal starts with *mezze*, small plates of hot or cold appetizers such as hummus, pickled vegetables, spicy sausages, or stuffed grape leaves. Main dishes include different types of kebab and *kibbeh*, a paste made of

Special Occasions

Throughout the Middle East, food plays an important part in special occasions such as religious festivals and family celebrations. In Iran, families prepare for the New Year festival, called Nowruz, by growing *sabzeh*—sprouting lentils or wheat seeds. The green shoots of these seeds are one of the items found on *haft sin*—the traditional table that is set with seven items that each symbolize something different. *Sabzeh* represent "new growth." For Jews, Passover is one of the main festivals of the religious year. They celebrate with a special meal, called a *seder*, at which every food has a special symbolic significance. For example, bitter herbs remind the Jews of the time their ancestors, the Israelites, spent as slaves in Egypt.

A special table is laid with sacred foods for the festival of Nowruz in Iran. You can see the *sabzeh* on the left. Candles are lit as a symbol of fire, and the fish are symbols of life.

lamb and **bulgur wheat** that is fried or baked, often with pine nuts, and served with a yogurt sauce. *Tabouleh*, a salad made from bulgur wheat, onions, tomatoes, and parsley, is also very popular. Every meal is served with bread.

Iran

Traditions of Persian cuisine vary considerably from those of the rest of the Middle East. The Iranian diet is based on rice, bread, fresh fruits and vegetables, and meats such as duck and goose, as well as lamb and chicken. Thick meat stews are served with rice; one of the oldest stew recipes is for a rich duck stew that has a sauce made from pomegranates and walnuts. Soups, called *aash*, are also popular. Tea is served with all meals throughout the day, and *dugh*, a type of yogurt drink, is also very popular. Traditionally, women have been highly regarded as cooks in Iran, and home-made food is still much prized and valued.

CHAPTER 6

Language and Literature

Arabic is the official language of all the countries of the Middle East except for Israel and Iran. In Israel, Hebrew is the official language, although Arabic is used officially for the Arab minority in the country. In Iran, Persian, sometimes called Farsi, is the official language. However, there are many other languages spoken in the Middle East including Kurdish, Turkish, Armenian, and the many Berber dialects.

Arabic

Arabic is the language of the Koran, and, because of that, it has a special significance for all Muslims. They believe that the Koran is a written record of the revelations from God to the Prophet Muhammad, recorded exactly as Muhammad received them, with not one word altered or added. They believe, therefore, that the Koran is the literal word of God. Although translations from Arabic into other languages are permitted, Muslims believe that the full meaning can only be understood by reading and reciting the Koran in the original Arabic. The language of the Koran is often known as classical or literary Arabic, and, although it is no longer spoken today, it provides the basis for modern Arabic.

"Modern standard Arabic" is the name given to the Arabic language that is used today. In practice, although many Arabs speak and write modern standard Arabic in formal situations, they actually communicate in one of the many dialects of Arabic. Major Arabic dialects include the versions spoken in Iraq, Egypt, Syria, and Saudi Arabia. Variations of dialects may

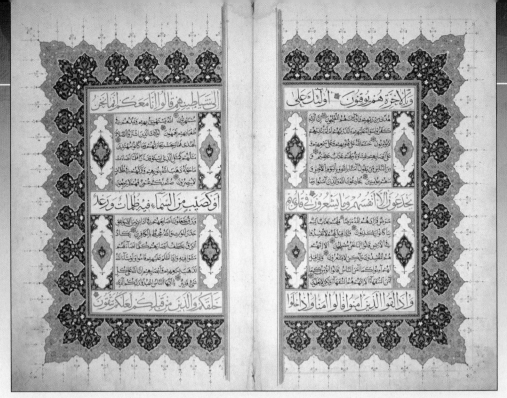

Two exquisitely decorated pages from a 16th century Persian Koran. Because it was forbidden to decorate the Koran with pictures, the creators of the Islamic holy book lavished their care upon the borders and the text itself.

even be found within some countries, which means it is possible for speakers from different parts of the Arabic-speaking world not to understand each other. However, as communication methods such as the Internet and mobile phones become increasingly widespread and as education improves, some of the extreme differences between Arabic dialects are disappearing.

Hebrew

Hebrew is the principal language spoken in Israel, used mainly by the country's large Jewish population. Biblical Hebrew was the language in which the Jewish holy book, the Torah, was written and was the language of the early Jewish people. But as Jewish communities spread around the world, many Jews began to speak the languages of the countries in which they lived. Hebrew gradually became the language of Jewish prayer and literature only. The revival of Hebrew as a modern spoken language began in the nineteenth century, when a Russian named Eliezer Ben-Yehuda emigrated to the region of Palestine and began to use Hebrew in everyday life. When Israel became a country in 1948, a modernized version of Hebrew became its official language.

Oral Traditions

From the earliest times, traditions of reciting and storytelling have been deeply rooted in the Middle East. Before the Koran was written down, the Prophet Muhammad and his followers learned the revelations of God by heart and recited them word for word. The tradition of learning the Koran by heart has not died out. Someone who can recite the complete Koran is still held in high esteem in Muslim society and is known as *hafiz*— "one who memorizes."

Storytellers were very popular in ancient times in the Middle East, and the best storytellers traveled from place to place telling their tales for a living. Even when writing systems began to be developed, the traditions of memorizing and telling stories did not die out because many people could neither read nor write.

Ancient Literature

Before the start of Islam, the earliest forms of literature in the Arab world were poems. Often these *qasidahs* (odes) described

This 14th-century Persian illustration shows a doctor visiting his patient, a scene from the *maqamat* of Al-Hariri (c.1054–1122) of Basra, which was extremely popular in the Islamic world for many centuries.

scenes and events from nomadic life. From this early poetic tradition came elaborate court poetry, which celebrated life at court and heaped praise and flattery on rulers. This poetry took hold at cultural centers such as Baghdad, where court poets were highly respected. Another popular type of literary work was the *maqamat*, a collection of dramatic stories told by a character who pokes fun at people from all levels of society.

Literature Today

Today, Cairo and Beirut are the literary centers of the Middle East. Probably the best-known writer from the Middle East is the Lebanese poet Kahlil Gibran (1883–1931). The poetic essays that make up Gibran's *The Prophet* have become well known around the world. The Egyptian writer Naguib Mahfouz (1911–) won the Nobel Prize for fiction in 1988.

A Thousand and One Nights

The Middle East has given the world some of its best-loved stories, many of which are still told in different forms today. "Aladdin," "Sinbad," and "Ali Baba and the Forty Thieves" are all tales from *A Thousand and One Nights*, also known as *The Arabian Nights*. This vast collection of stories dates from ancient times, although the stories that are known to us today are set mainly in Baghdad, Cairo, and Damascus. All the stories have the same introduction: the king Shahrayar sleeps with a different girl every night and has her executed in the morning. But the cunning Sharazad tells the king a different story every night and leaves it uncompleted, so every morning the king is forced to keep her alive to find out how the story ends.

CHAPTER 7

Arts

The Middle East was the cradle of civilization—the center of some of the world's earliest and greatest civilizations. Not surprisingly, it has a vast and rich history of architecture, art, music, and crafts. After the sixth century A.D., much of the region's culture stemmed from the Islamic religion.

Architecture

From the pyramids of Egypt and the ruins of ancient Persepolis in Iran to the modern designs of the latest hotels in the Gulf states, architecture in the Middle East is both varied and stunning. When the Arab armies began to spread the new religion of Islam from the Arabian peninsula, their first in priority once they had taken control of a place was to establish a place of worship—a mosque. During the Umayyad dynasty (A.D. 661–750), the first great monuments of Islam were constructed—the Great Mosque of Damascus, in Syria, and the Dome of the Rock, in Jerusalem.

The Muslim builders adopted some of the styles of the people they had conquered. Among these were the Byzantines.

The Pyramids

These huge structures were built by the pharaohs (kings) and queens of Egypt to house their bodies after death. The most famous of these are probably the pyramids of Giza, located just outside Cairo, which were the royal burial places for the capital of ancient Egypt, Memphis. The size of these pyramids is staggering. It is estimated that the Great Pyramid, tomb of Khufu (who reigned from 2589–2566 B.C.) contains over two million blocks of stone.

The Dome of the Rock in Jerusalem is one of the holiest sites in the Islamic world. It was built in the 7th century. The dome is clad in gold, and its walls are decorated with stunning mosaics that incorporate quotations from the Koran.

They covered walls with beautiful marble and mosaic decorations. In the Great Mosque of Damascus, they also set a semicircular alcove (*mihrab*) into one wall to indicate the direction of prayer (*qiblah*) for all Muslims. The *mihrab* quickly became a feature of mosques throughout the Islamic lands.

As the Islamic Empire expanded, and as different rulers came and went from power, distinctive styles of architecture developed. In Egypt, the **Fatimids** built the al-Azhar mosque in the tenth century. This became a center of learning, and al-Azhar University is claimed today to be the oldest university in the world. In Persia, the ruler of the **Safavids**, Shah Abbas (ruled 1588–1629) chose the majestic city of Isfahan, with its huge central square and beautiful domed mosques covered in patterned and colored tiles, as his new capital.

New Styles

Modern architecture in the Middle East has been taken to new levels in the wealthy Gulf states. Architects designing luxurious, ultramodern hotels in the United Arab Emirates have experimented with exciting and new ideas. For example, the elegant Jumeira Beach Hotel is designed in the form of a breaking wave. The tallest hotel in the world, the Burj al-Arab, stands on its own manmade island just off the coast of Dubai. It is in the shape of a billowing sail and rises to a height of 1,050 feet (320 meters).

Music and Dance

The love of poetry and the spoken word in the Arab world has led to the important place held by song in Arab music. Singers such as the Egyptian Umm Kulthum and the Lebanese Fairouz were once superstars in the Middle East and are still immensely popular. Fairouz was popular in the 1960s and 1970s. Umm Kulthum, known as the "Nightingale of the East" in Egypt, found fame from the 1940s through the 1960s and often sang songs that were up to an hour long, elaborating and **improvising** around a melody.

The role of music in Islam is widely debated. Some Muslims believe that while vocal music is acceptable, instrumental music is not. In Muslim worship, the call to prayer, or **adhan**, which is given five times a day, is not considered music, nor are prayers themselves or recitation of the Koran.

Umm Kulthum

"When she sang, she was never the heroine. People heard their own story in her songs."

Amal Fahmy, Egyptian radio commentator, about Umm Kulthum.

These Kurdish women are performing a traditional line dance at a wedding in Halabja, Iraq.

Calligraphy

Muslims consider calligraphy—the art of beautiful writing—to be the most precious of all arts. It is the means by which the Koran, which Muslims believe to be the literal word of God, is transmitted, so great care is taken to make the writing as perfect as possible. Over time, different styles of calligraphy developed, some suitable for large-scale decoration on a building, others used for highly decorated copies of the Koran. Calligraphy continues to be an important part of Muslim culture today, with calligraphers such as the Iraqi Hassan Massoudy combining centuries-old traditions with new ideas and influences.

Belly dancing (*raqs sharqi*) has a history that goes back to ancient Egyptian times, and it is the most famous dance style of the region. Belly dancers perform in Cairo, and many performers are big stars. Although state and religious disapproval led to a ban on foreign belly dancers in Egypt in 2003, the restriction was lifted two years later. In 2006, Hamas also announced that it would ban belly dancing in the **Palestinian National Authority**. Other dances are associated with celebrations such as weddings. The *hagallah*, for example, originally comes from Libya but is performed in western Egypt. It involves a veiled woman who dances along a line of chanting and clapping men, and it takes place before a wedding procession begins.

Crafts

In the past, workshops throughout the Islamic world were kept busy by wealthy Muslim rulers who demanded the finest carpets and textiles, highly elaborate glass and metalwork, and beautifully decorated pottery. From the beginning of Islam, Muslims avoided the representation of living beings on any religious buildings, because it was considered that the creation of living things was unique to God. This led to the development of highly ornate geometric and floral patterns which were used to decorate everything from carpets to mosque walls. Calligraphy was often also incorporated into this style of decoration.

CHAPTER 8

Issues for the Future

The people of the Middle East are renowned for their warmth, friendliness, and hospitality. The vast majority of the region's inhabitants live peaceful lives, working, bringing up their children, and enjoying their normal day-to-day existences. Yet, a brief look at headlines in the newspapers will show that there are still many ethnic and religious conflicts to be resolved in the region.

The Kurds

The Kurds have frequently found themselves under pressure to abandon their Kurdish identity and conform to the ways of life of the countries in which they live. For example, in Turkey, the Kurdish language was banned for many years. Repression of the Kurds has been particularly brutal in Iraq. During the war between Iraq and Iran in the 1980s, some Iraqi Kurds fought with the Iranians. After the war, Iraqi leader Saddam Hussein took his revenge on the Kurds by launching chemical attacks against Kurdish villages. Thousands of Kurds died, and many thousands more are still suffering from the long-term effects of these attacks.

Today, after the removal of Saddam Hussein by the U.S.-led coalition in 2003, the future for the Iraqi Kurds looks more hopeful, as Iraqi Kurds form the second largest block in the Iraqi parliament. In addition, a Kurd, Jalal Talabani, became Iraq's president in 2005.

The Future for Women

The role of women in Middle Eastern society is changing, but, in general, women still have fewer opportunities in education and in the workplace than men. In many places, the strong Muslim traditions of keeping men and women segregated have made it difficult for women to go out to work. However, in countries such as Kuwait, where women recently gained the right to vote, or Jordan, where women are being actively encouraged to enter the political life of the country, the future looks more hopeful.

The bill on women's **suffrage** was passed on May 16, 2005 in the Kuwaiti parliament, and brought an end to a 40-year campaign to allow women to vote in Kuwait. Kuwait is the fourth of the Gulf states to allow women to vote, after Bahrain, Oman, and Qatar. Saudi Arabia does not have female suffrage. In June 2005, the Kuwaiti parliament welcomed its first female minister, Massouma al-Mubarak, who was appointed minister of planning and administrative development.

Watched by her personal bodyguard, Awaz Abdulwahid Khidir talks on her mobile phone. Awaz is a member of the Kurdistan Democratic Party, and was recently elected to be one of a handful of new female mayors in Iraqi Kurdistan.

Israelis and Palestinians

One of the Middle Eastern conflicts dominating the headlines is that between the Israelis and the Palestinians. This struggle, as noted earlier, currently focuses on two pieces of territory: the Gaza Strip, which is a section of Mediterranean coastal plain, and the West Bank, a hilly region to the west of the Jordan River. Although Israel withdrew its settlements from the Gaza Strip in the summer of 2005, the West Bank and East Jerusalem remain disputed territories. Many Israeli Jews support the end of occupation of the West Bank, and the relocation of the Israeli settlers who had made their homes there, as part of the peace process. However, more radical Jewish settlers see the withdrawal from the occupied territories as a betrayal by the Israeli government.

After the death of the Palestinian leader Yasser Arafat in 2004, Mahmoud Abbas was elected president of the Palestinian National Authority. This change in leadership seemed as if it might bring new possibilities for peace between Israel and the Palestinians. But plans for Palestinian statehood—and the future of millions of Palestinian refugees—remain unclear. In January 2006, the first elections for the new Palestinian Legislative Council resulted in 76 of the 132 seats going to the Palestinian militant organization Hamas. Because Hamas is regarded as a terrorist organization by many countries—including Israel, the United States, and the countries of the European Union—this election result has complicated negotiations in the peace process. In order for the peace process to continue, the countries involved in mediating between Israel and the Palestinians have called on Hamas to renounce violence, express support for the peace process, and recognize Israel's right to exist. Hamas has responded by calling these demands "unfair." The future remains uncertain.

Choice of Peace

"The only way is the choice of peace. It is impossible to liberate Palestine with the use of weapons because the balance of power is not with us."

Mahmoud Abbas, President of the Palestinian National Authority.

Meeting in Music

In August 2005, a landmark concert sent a strong message to the world of the desire for peace between Jews and Arabs in the Middle East region. The concert was given by the West-Eastern Divan Orchestra in Ramallah, a town in the West Bank that is the headquarters for the Palestinian National Authority and has been a flashpoint for violence between Israelis and Palestinians. The orchestra is made up of musicians from Israel, the Palestinian National Authority, Egypt, Syria, Jordan, and Lebanon. It was founded by Edward Said, a Palestinian-American writer and scholar who died in 2003, and Daniel Barenboim, an Argentinian-born Jewish musician who moved to Israel in 1953 and has long worked for peace in the region.

Members of the West-Eastern Divan Orchestra acknowledge the applause of the audience at the groundbreaking concert in Ramallah in 2005.

MIDDLE EAST: POPULATION STATISTICS

NAME	POPULATION	ETHNICITIES	RELIGIONS
Bahrain	688,345* (includes 235,108 nonnationals)	Arab 62%, non-Bahraini 38%	Muslim (Shi'a and Sunni) 81%, Christian 9%, other 10%
Egypt	77,505,756*	Arab 99%, Greek, Nubian, Armenian 1%	Muslim (mostly Sunni) 94%, Coptic Christian and other 6%
Iran	68,017,860*	Persian 51%, Azeri 24%, Gilaki and Mazandarani 8%, Kurd 7%, Arab 3%, Lur 2%, Baloch 2%, Turkmen 2%, other 1%	Shi'a Muslim 89%, Sunni Muslim 9%, other 2%
Iraq	26,074,906*	Arab 75%–80%, Kurdish 15%–20%, Turkoman, Assyrian, or other 5%	Muslim 97% (Shi'a 60%–65%, Sunni 32%–37%), Christian, or other 3%
Israel	6,276,883	Jewish 76%, non-Jewish 24% (mostly Arab)	Jewish 76%, Muslim 16%, Christian 2%, Druze 2%, other 4%
Jordan	5,759,732*	Arab 98%, Circassian 1%, Armenian 1%	Sunni Muslim 92%, Christian 6%, other 2%
Kuwait	2,335,648* (includes 1,291,354 nonnationals)	Kuwaiti Arab 45%, other Arab 35%, South Asian 9%, Iranian 4%, other 7%	Muslim 85% (Sunni 59.5%, Shi'a 25.5%), Christian, Hindu, Parsi, and other 15%
Lebanon	3,826,018*	Arab 95%, Armenian 4%, other 1%	Muslim 60%, Christian 39%, other 1%
Libya	5,765,563* (includes 166,510 nonnationals)	Berber and Arab 97%, other 3%	Sunni Muslim 97%, other 3%
Oman	3,001,583* (includes 577,293 nonnationals)	Arab, Baluchi, South Asian (Indian, Pakistani, Sri Lankan, Bangladeshi), African	Ibadi Muslim 75%, Sunni Muslim, Shi'a Muslim, and Hindu 25%
PNA[†] (Gaza Strip)	1,376,289*	Palestinian Arab and other Arab 100%	Muslim 99%, Christian 1%
(West Bank)	2,385,615 (2004 estimate)	Palestinian Arab and other 83%, Jewish 17%	Muslim 75%, Jewish 17%, Christian and other 8%
Qatar	863,051*	Arab 40%, Pakistani 18%, Indian 18%, Iranian 10%, other 14%	Muslim 95%, other 5%
Saudi Arabia	26,417,599* (includes 5,576,076 nonnationals)	Arab 90%, Afro-Asian 10%	Sunni Muslim 85%, Shi'a Muslim 15%
Syria	18,448,752	Arab 90%, Kurds, Armenians, and other 10%	Sunni Muslim 74%, other Muslim 16%, Christian 10%
UAE	2,563,212* (inc. est. 1,606,079 nonnationals)	Emiri 19%, other Arab and Iranian 23%, South Asian 50%, other expatriates (includes Westerners and East Asians) 8%	Muslim 96%, Christian, Hindu, and other 4%
Yemen	20,727,063*	Arab 95%, Afro-Arab 3%, South Asians, Europeans 2%	Sunni Muslim 55%, Shi'a Muslim 42%, Jewish, Christian, and Hindu 3%

Sources: CIA World Factbook; Financial Times World Desk Reference

*(2005 estimates)
[†]Palestinian National Authority

GLOSSARY

Abbasid dynasty: the Muslim dynasty that ruled the Islamic empire from 750–1258, although its power declined from the tenth century onward

adhan: the Muslim call to prayer, usually given from a tall tower on a mosque called a minaret

Arabian Peninsula: the large area of land surrounded on three sides by the Red Sea, Arabian Sea, and Persian Gulf

bulgur wheat: a form of whole wheat that has been partly cooked during processing, making it easy to use in recipes

dialect: a version of a language usually associated with a particular region

dowry: money or property given before a marriage, either by the man's family to the wife, or brought by the wife to her husband through their marriage

Fatimids: the Shi'a dynasty that held power in Egypt from 969–1171

Gaza Strip: the 140-square-mile (360 sq km) region bordered by Israel, Egypt, and the Mediterranean Sea that was occupied by Israel 1967-2005 and is part of the Palestinian National Authority

Hajj: the pilgrimage to Mecca that must be undertaken at least once in a lifetime by Muslims who are healthy and who can afford it

harem: the women's quarters in a Muslim house

improvise: to make something up as you go along, without previous planning

irrigation: the process of distributing water to land in order to grow crops

Islam: one of the world's three major monotheistic (one God) religions (along with Christianity and Judaism), founded in the seventh century by the Prophet Muhammad

Judaism: one of the world's three major monotheistic (one God) religions (along with Christianity and Islam)

Ka'bah: the cube structure in Mecca to which all Muslims direct their prayer

Koran: the sacred text of Islam, considered by Muslims to contain the revelations of God to Muhammad

literacy: the ability to read and write

Mesopotamian provinces: the lowlands watered by the Tigris and Euphrates rivers during the time of the Ottoman Empire

migration: the movement of people or animals from one place to another

mosque: a Muslim place of worship

Muslim: a follower of Islam

GLOSSARY

nomads: people who move from place to place with no fixed home, often to look for fresh grazing for their herds of animals

oases: fertile places in deserts

Ottoman Empire: the empire of the Ottoman Turks, which lasted over 600 years (1299–1922), and which included all of the Middle East except Iran and the desert interior of Arabia

Palestinian National Authority: the Palestinian government organization that controls the Gaza Strip and West Bank, established in 1993

patriarch: a leader of the Coptic church

population density: the average number of people living in a square mile (or square kilometer)

prophet: someone through whom God is believed to speak

Safavids: the dynasty of Shi'a Muslims who ruled Iran from A.D. 1502–1736

sect: a group within a religion

suffrage: the right to vote

Torah: the first five books of the Hebrew Scriptures, which are sacred to Jews

Umayyad dynasty: the first Muslim dynasty, based in Damascus, that ruled from A.D. 661–750

urbanization: movement of people from rural areas to live and work in cities

West Bank: the 2,263-square-mile (5,860 sq km) region west of the Jordan River between Israel and Jordan that has been occupied by Israel since 1967 and is part of the Palestinian National Authority

Zoroastrian: following Zoroastrianism, a religion that started in Persia with the teachings of the prophet Zoroaster

FURTHER RESOURCES

Websites

Arab Culture and Civilization-Audio/Video.
   http://arabworld.nitle.org/audiovisual.php?module
Sinai: The Bedouin Way
   www.geographia.com/egypt/sinai/bedouin02.htm
Jewish Virtual Library-Society and Culture
   www.jewishvirtuallibrary.org/jsource/vie/viesoctoc.html
MidEastWeb-The Arts
   www.mideastweb.org/culture.htm

Note to educators and parents: The publisher has carefully reviewed these Web sites to ensure that they are suitable for children. Many Web sites change frequently, however, and Gareth Stevens, Inc., cannot guarantee that a site's future contents will continue to meet our high standards of quality and educational value. Be advised that children should be closely supervised whenever they access the Internet.

Books

Cannuyer, Christian. *Coptic Eygpt: Christians of the Nile* (Discoveries). Harry N Abrams, 2001.
Gelletly, Leeanne. *The Kurds* (The Growth and Influence in the Nations of Asia and Central Asia). Mason Crest Publishers, 2005.
Millard, Anne. *The Great Pyramid of Giza* (Places in History). World Almanac Library, 2005.
Sheen, Barbara. *Foods of Iran* (A Taste of Culture). KidHaven Press, 2006.

ABOUT THE AUTHOR

Nicola Barber is the author of many children's non-fiction books specializing in geography, history, and the arts.

ABOUT THE CONSULTANT

William Ochsenwald is Professor of History at Virginia Polytechnic Institute and State University. He is author of *The Middle East: A History*, a textbook now in its sixth edition. Professor Ochsenwald has also written many other books and articles dealing with the history of the Middle East.

INDEX